Le Maestro

A Holocaust survivors' tale

Inspired by a true story

First Edition

By NC Arca

Copyright © 2025 by Nicanor C. Arca

All rights reserved.

No part of this publication may be reproduced, distributed, or transmitted in any form or by any means, including photocopying, recording, or other electronic or mechanical methods, without the prior written permission of the author.

Paperback ISBN: 979-8-9942082-0-5

Hardback: ISBN: 979-8-9942082-1-2

E-Book ISBN : 979-8-9942082-2-9

Book cover design and artwork by:

Nicanor C Arca

Table of Contents:

Disclaimer: ……………………….i

Dedications:……………………….ii

Acknowledgements:…………………iv

Preface:………………………….vi

Introduction:………………………viii

Chapter 1, Perspective……………….1

Chapter 2, The uncanny meeting……..5

Chapter 3, Prague…………………12

Chapter 4, Escape to France…………22

Chapter 5, Paris…………………...26

Chapter 6, Exodus………………...33

Chapter 7, Delivery………………..37

Chapter 8, Narrow Escape………….42

Chapter 9, Larzac Plateau…………...52

Chapter 10, Post-War……………...58

Chapter 11, Departure……………..61

Chapter 12, Conclusion……………..66

Disclaimer:

This book is a work of creative non-fiction and is based on actual events and is portrayed to the best of the author's present recollections, experiences, and research. While most of the stories in this book are true, some names, identifying details, events, dates, and characters have been changed to protect the privacy and the anonymity of the people involved. In some instances, people, places, timelines, and conversations have been recreated for narrative purposes.

The author has to the best of his abilities to attempt to ensure the information in this book is consistent and complete. The book is not indented as a substitute for professional advice (legal, medical, historical, etc.). The author specifically disclaims all responsibility for any liability, loss, harm, damage, or personal affliction of any nature that is incurred consequently, direct, or indirectly, of the use and application of any content of this book.

Dedications:

This book is dedicated to all essential healthcare workers, particularly CNAs (certified nursing assistants).

These are the people who selflessly work shifts that cover the needs of the most vulnerable patients twenty-four hours a day, seven days a week, on weekends, holidays and even on their personal days. They care for those who cannot care for themselves, individuals that their families, friends or relatives cannot care for due to the need for a higher level of care and special needs of these patients. These special individuals care for our elderly, incapacitated, mentally challenged, and people with disabilities and others. They provide medical care, feed, shower, and dress them on a daily basis.

Some of the challenges they endure are caring for patients who refuse to be cared for. At times I have witnessed them endure physically, verbal assaults, at times discriminatory and racial attacks. Yet they do not have the right to complain or litigate. Another saddening truth is that at times health care workers are victims of false accusations. Do not get me wrong, not all health care workers are saints, but most are honest caring good people. In most situations they just keep to themselves for fear of losing their livelihood, being deported and not being able to provide financial support to their families locally and abroad.

These workers are truly the unsung heroes; they are the most underpaid and underappreciated workers. I hope this book brings awareness and enlightenment to the readers that they may understand and acknowledge their work. If you ever meet them, please show them the respect and appreciation they deserve.

In honor of our health care workers, a part of the proceeds from this book will go to charities that support employees of long-term care facilities, group homes, dementia units, and our overseas charities and support rural and indigent children's hospitals.

Also, may this book raise awareness to increase government funding for our most vulnerable and frail population. I have seen the decline and neglect that most of our senior citizens are experiencing today. I hope that in some way we will help make a difference.

Acknowledgements:

I want to give thanks to:

My wife, Anna, my daughter Nicole, and son Bradley for their unwavering support.

To my late father, Joselito Arca, who has taught me honesty, humility and moral principles that guide me to this day.

To my mother, Corazon Intano-Arca. My siblings, Joe, Annie, and Angelo Arca for the support given to me throughout my life.

To my Aunties, Mama Fin, Auntie Mel, Auntie Baby and Auntie Nene who helped during my college days.

To Nina Encarnacion, Jim and Jeff of the Industrial clinic in Detroit, for giving me my first medical job in the US.

To My good friend Brent Flesner for his support during the tough times in Detroit, Michigan.

To Dr. Funderburke and the faculty at the University of Florida Jacksonville Family Medicine program.

To Mr. Torman., who helped and inspired me to continue writing this story.

To Mr. Rick Hutto, whose invaluable advice gave me the insights and advice to complete this book.

To April McFadden for her feedback on this book.

To Zoe and Myka Char for helping me edit this book.

To to all the people who help me throughout my life's journey.

Lastly to God almighty for the blessing he has gifted me.

Preface:

As a Physician with more than 30 years' experience in taking care of dementia patients, I can attest that majority of patients will exhibit some sort of memory deficits. Even though many patients have a cluster of symptoms, every individual is different. I have observed that dementia patients' cognition and memory can turn like the tide; memory and mental clarity comes and goes without precedence and is unpredictable. Sometimes a dementia patient can be very confused, incoherent, delirious, and worse combative.

Then there are moments when they can be fully lucid and carry on a normal rational conversation, as if they did not have dementia at all. This occurs randomly and it is not possible to predict when it will happen. Most of the time dementia symptoms worsen in the afternoon or early evening, this is termed "Sundowning." *

Most dementia patients have short term memory deficits, like what they ate for breakfast or what happened just two hours ago. And most of the time their old memories stay intact, examples, like where they went to high school or specific events that happened while they were growing up. Although not all cases of dementia are the same. Some severe cases there is total loss of cognition and self-awareness. In this story, one of my patients had this moment of lucidity. She vividly recalled and was able to narrate a lot about the events that happened in her remote past.

References:

https://www.alz.org

Introduction:

This is a story of how I met a patient, one hundred and two-year-old woman, and promised to fulfill her request, before she left this world.

" The world should know," she uttered, "let the world know" what she and the millions of victims of the Holocaust experienced during the second world war.

This patient had an existing condition of Alzheimer's Dementia. She had ongoing Dementia symptoms although for some divine intervention she had these moments of lucidity and was able to vividly recall her remarkable story of how she and her husband escaped and survived the Holocaust. Weeks later sadly she passed away. She requested me to share her story of their hardships during the Nazi occupation of most of Europe during World War two. She describes in detail how they fled their hometown of Prague, in the Czech Republic and manage to reach France where they elusively evaded capture from the Nazi's Gestapo on several occasions. As the war went on for years, she and her husband were one of the lucky ones to survive hiding in the shadows of the Nazi regime.

Both gifted with pulchritudinous physical appearance, intelligence, and talent gave them an advantage to survive throughout the time of the war. As their journey in life was not at all easy even in the post war era they pursued on and lived a long and remarkable life.

Chapter 1

Perspective

This story begins in all places in the Philippines circa 1995. "Help! Help! Someone Help! My son cannot breathe! Someone please," shouts from a young father who came running from a Jeepney into the Emergency room. In his arms, he carried his 7-year-old son. The young boy's head was slumped over, arms dangling and his face pale, and lips turning blue.

Doctors and nurses in the emergency room hurried to help the child, placing him on a stretcher and administering high-flow oxygen while inserting intravenous lines; for now, the young boy remained stable.

I was a young eager fourth year medical student experiencing a true emergency for the first time. The pediatric rotation was my first rotation as a student, once full of confidence; it seemed all the knowledge I had as a student was to no avail. "Dr Arca" yelled Dr. Perez our senior pediatric resident, as he ordered Me to call Dr. Diaz the pediatric intern that day and ordered us admit the patient to pediatric ward. Dr. Perez remained in the emergency room, overwhelmed by a constant stream of pediatric traumas, urgent deliveries, and various other emergencies.

The boy had difficulty from the start; he should have been intubated and put on a ventilator immediately. Although back then most hospitals faced a shortage of ventilators, so they were allocated exclusively to patients in intensive care units. We used to intubate patients and manually ventilate them with oxygen in eight-hour shifts as interns, especially for pediatric cases. And once this happens, the chances of survival are slim to none.

The boys' breathing worsened, now rapid and swallowed; the little boy was just gasping for air.

He experienced an abrupt onset of coughing, followed by cyanosis and cessation of respirations. His father and mother urgently exclaimed that he was not breathing. Do something, Dr. Diaz was trying to intubate the boy, while I tried to force air using an outdated leaking airbag, he was exhausted and tiring out, and just like that he took his last breath and died. The father yelled out No! No! No!

Just then Dr. Perez came running up from the emergency room and faced the grim reality.

The father ran furious towards him and choked him, shouting at him "you let my son die." Dr. Diaz and I pulled them apart as emotions flared in the pediatric ward.

The father pulled out a picture of the young boy and held it towards our faces. He said in his crying voice, "this is my boy, you could not save him, and now you cannot bring him back! He is gone!"

The mother was pulling him away from us, as she was in a state of shock. The chaos calmed down and reality set in.

The pediatric ward atmosphere was so cold. It was hard to describe the feeling, I did feel guilty that I could not do anything to save the young boy, although I really could not do anything as a student. I felt bad for Dr. Perez, although he was busy handling other emergencies in the emergency room and was not there when the boy coded, he still had to take responsibility for what happened. Surprisingly, Dr Diaz seemed unfazed by everything. As the evening went on, we managed several more cases, although it was less complicated the evening felt so draining. As weeks passed on working in Hospital, I reflected on how fragile life can be and how blessed people who have lived their full long life.

Fast forward 30 years later, through many trials and tribulation, failures, and setbacks, I never expected to be where I am today. From working in the most underserved and poorest hospitals in the world to the most advanced medical centers in America. Through my experience, I have witnessed both the profound joy of birth and the sorrow of death, touching individuals across all ages and stages of life. I know and appreciate now the saying, "Health is wealth."

And throughout those experiences, one lesson I learned is that life you can hand you serendipity or zemblanity it is all on one's "perspective".

Chapter 2

The uncanny meeting.

It was a foggy morning, on a calm and cool winter morning in Central Florida, in 2017, the day after Christmas. Most city residents stayed indoors after the holiday weekend, so my commute was easy with hardly any traffic on the empty streets. But illness, accidents or emergencies do not take holidays or days off, so do physicians, nurses, and the hospital staff that keep it running. As I approached the Hospital grounds, which is a massive complex, covering at least four blocks of real estate in the heart of the city. I drove in a small hidden driveway that leads into a larger garage door, after a few swipes with my badge, access was finally granted, I drove in the dark damp humid fog-laden tunnel entrance that descends into the building's basement hospital parking garage.

I tried to motivate myself and feel optimistic hoping the day will go smoothly without any major problems this holiday weekend.

As I stepped foot on the parking garage and I walked towards the basement elevators, the petrichor emanating from the underground parking lot and the machinery sounds from the hospitals ventilation systems, prepped me for the calm before the storm.

I managed to get to main floor of the hospital, before me a long hallway now in sight, I can see the stretchers with people lined up along the halls, some moaning in pain, some shouting and cursing and then the overhead pages, that you need to be mindful of, but in the midst of all the hospital chaos, as a seasoned clinician all of it felt mellifluous.

I venture down the basement to the hospitalist's call-room; it is a cold musty room with flickering fluorescent lights and sticky floors. I picked up my patient list from the pile. The five-page patient list, my workday has begun. I scurry up the fire escape, as the elevators take too long. I headed to the physicians' lounge for a warm cup of coffee and the complimentary breakfast, a nice gesture from the hospital administration.

As is customary, following a brief discussion with several colleagues, I proceeded to begin my work promptly. As I walked down the hall, I browsed through my patient list and what cases, looks standard, thirty-two patients to start with.

As I started my daily round, I usually start out in the Emergency Room first to see the new admissions; I talk to the Emergency Room physicians about the admissions for the day. The hospital's front line, in the early mornings this department is little bit quiet; Then the Emergency Room tend to get chaotic during the evenings, patients rush in from motor vehicle accidents, gunshots, stoke alerts, heart attacks, pregnant and pediatric emergencies, everything and anything that arrives at the emergency doors the staff are ready to take care of. I aimed to wrap up my tasks ahead of the rush; after admitting several patients, I shift gears and make my way to the Intensive Care Unit. The ICU patients are more complex, extremely sick, and are most all on life support. Intensivists oversee patient care in this unit, and as hospitalists, we collaborate with them to manage patients until they leave the ICU. Today was a good day, no major complication in the ICU, so I move on…

I work my way through the medical-surgical wards, I mostly manage follow-ups and discharges for many patients. I spent almost half of my day in this department.

As the day winded down, my last stop was the Inpatient rehabilitation unit, a step-down from the hospital, less intense. Patients here are recovering from their acute problems, working on rehabilitation and physical therapy. Certain patients remain in the unit for extended periods, sometimes lasting several weeks. I only had four patients in that unit that day.

From my patient list I see one patient; room 717 was a one hundred- and two-years old woman. I thought this would be interesting, so I planned to see her last. It is uncommon to encounter individuals of this age group; they have witnessed significant historical events, from the 1930s through the Second World War and into the decades spanning the 1950s to the 1970s.

Their experiences show how the world changed during these times, and many have noteworthy stories. Upon review of her chart, the patient has been hospitalized for several days and exhibited mental status changes consistent with delirium, which is not uncommon given her history of dementia. However, she is now demonstrating notable improvement both physically and cognitively.

While searching for the nurse assigned to her, I noticed her presence. In a clear and audible manner, I asked, "Sino ang nurse nang pasyente sa seven seventeen" (who is the nurse for the patient in seven seventeen).

The nurse, upon hearing her native language spoken unexpectedly and loudly in the hospital corridor, was momentarily startled. Her initial shock gave way to amusement as she realized the situation. Turning toward me, she let out a hearty laugh, clearly finding humor in the unexpected exchange. In that brief moment, the tension eased, creating a sense of camaraderie between us as we both recognized the shared language and the uniqueness of the encounter.

I asked, "How's our patient in room 717?" She answered in her high-pitched Philippine accent, "Most of the time she's confused, doctor, but she can answer some basic questions and sometimes remains alert." I thanked her by saying, "Maraming Salamat," (Thank you very much), as I headed to the patient's room.

I made my way quietly down the foyer, searching for Room 717. Upon reaching the half-opened door, I gave it a gentle knock before stepping into the semi-darkened room. "Hello," I called out, but there was no immediate response. Raising my voice slightly, I announced, "This is the doctor." In response, I heard a faint moan—an indication that she was awake.

I opened the window blinds, allowing natural light to filter into the semi-darkened room. As daylight crept in, I observed that she remained groggy, her eyelids heavy, and her demeanor suggesting she was still quite sleepy. I paused for a moment to give her time to adjust to the change in brightness, ensuring the environment would be more comfortable for our interaction.

I started slowly, asking basic questions. "Do you know where you are?" She answers in a what I perceived sounded to me like a German accent. "I think I'm in the hospital and who are you?" Patient said. I tried to use the few German phrases. I said "guten tag". She lit up a bit, as I continued... "Wie heist du" She was awakening a bit more and slowly became more alert, and She answers me in German, "Mien Name ist Rebecca Frolich" and then followed by a few rapid German sentences that I did not understand. I said "Nien, ich spreche kein Deutch" (I do not speak German) She smirks, she is more alert now, I did not expect much, but this was a good start. I asked her "spreche Sie English," she said with a hard accent "I do," I was relieved as I was running out to German phrases to say, so we continued to converse in English.

I continued asking her some questions at her bedside, "Rebecca are you, German?" Her facial expression changed, as if she was angry at me, then she said "No! I am not German" She said, "I'm Czechoslovakian."

I realized I had misinterpreted Rebecca's accent, and my assumption had unintentionally upset her when I asked if she was German. As someone deeply interested in history, I considered her age and recognized that she must have lived through World War II. Since she was not German, it became clear that she was a survivor from wartime the Czech Republic. I imagined that she must have an incredibly compelling story to share if her memory allowed.

I inquired, "Where were you during the war?" She turned towards me, her demeanor noticeably brightening with apparent enthusiasm to share her experience.

At first, she was trying to gather and find words to say, and now she is slowly becoming more alert as she goes on.

As mentioned before, most dementia patients retain and remember old memories, I tried to keep her focused, as I kept quiet, no distractions and I listened intently.

"I will tell you a story" Her deep elderly voice.

Rebecca looked at me solemnly and said, "It was a terrible time. We lost all our families during the war. I was the only one that survived." Her voice carried both pain and strength, and with a profound sense of conviction, she added, "The world should know of my story." Hearing these words sent a chill down my spine, the gravity of her experience suddenly became very real and present.

Moved by her declaration, I quietly pulled up a chair and sat at her bedside. I remained silent a rare occurrence in the midst of my daily routine, but Rebecca's story compelled me to pause everything else. I was deeply interested in what she would share, so I stayed, attentive and ready to listen.

Chapter 3

Prague.

This is Rebecca's story...

She starts telling me how she grew up in a middle-class Jewish family in Prague, Czech Republic. She recalls Prague as a modern, vibrant city at the time, diverse and mixed with Jews, Roman Catholics, Protestants and Russian orthodox. The city was inclusive without religious prejudice.

Rebecca graduated from Carles University in Prague, where she earned a degree in history. Her academic achievements were complemented by her fluency in five languages, a skill that would later prove invaluable in the changing times.

It was during her college years that Rebecca met her future husband, Hugo Frolich. She described Hugo as tall and slender, standing about six feet two inches, with dark hair and striking blue eyes. Rebecca recalled, with a touch of humor, that she was considered "beautiful" as well, a memory she shared jokingly during her testimony.

Rebecca reflected on her younger years, mentioning, "I was smaller, had blonde hair and blue eyes back then." These memories seemed to carry a touch of nostalgia, painting a vivid image of her appearance during that time in her life.

She went on to describe her wedding to Hugo, recalling that they were married in a small, traditional Jewish ceremony attended by their closest family and friends. The occasion was intimate and heartfelt, surrounded by loved ones who celebrated their union.

Following their marriage, Hugo completed his college education and began to pursue his passion for music. He established himself as a talented conductor and composer, known for his remarkable skills as a multi-instrumentalist. Hugo possessed a captivating baritone voice that, as Rebecca fondly noted, "never misses a note." His career flourished as he primarily conducted performances at the Opera House of Prague, while also traveling to other cities throughout the Czech region to share his musical talents. After finishing college, Rebecca pursued her profession as a schoolteacher. Life was serene, until the dawn of the war.

Rebecca goes on to recall her memories of the early 1930s, a time when the Nazi party was rapidly gaining power in Germany. She describes how, as the Nazis rose to prominence, their antisemitic rhetoric became increasingly widespread and influential. This growing wave of hatred did not remain confined within Germany's borders. Instead, the Nazi party's influence and the associated tide of antisemitism began to spread throughout Europe, casting a shadow over neighboring countries and affecting the lives of Jewish communities far beyond Germany itself.

Disturbing reports of Jewish persecution spread rapidly throughout Europe, with incidents increasing across Germany, Austria, Poland, Russia, and reaching into the Czech Republic.

Around 1939, the situation in Czechoslovakia took a dire turn. Nazi Germany first invaded the Sudetenland region, and within approximately five months, German forces extended their occupation to the rest of the Czech lands. As a result, Prague, Rebecca's home, came under Nazi rule, marking the beginning of a dark and oppressive era for Jewish communities and the city as a whole.

Rebecca vividly remembers the implementation of a particularly dehumanizing regulation imposed upon the Jewish community: all Jews were required to wear the Star of David on their clothing. This visible badge was not merely a symbol; it served as an unmistakable identifier, marking Jewish individuals in public spaces. The intent behind this mandate was to make it easier for Nazi authorities and local collaborators to single out, monitor, and harass Jewish people.

The Star of David badge became an instrument of systematic discrimination. It facilitated the segregation of Jews from the rest of the population and was a precursor to even more severe measures. Over time, this visible mark enabled authorities to locate and eventually round up Jews for deportation, contributing to the widespread persecution and suffering experienced by Rebecca, her family, and the entire Jewish community during this dark period. *

She also stated that once arrested they were either sent to the Ghettos or to the concentration camps. During this period of mounting danger and uncertainty, Hugo and Rebecca came to the realization that remaining in Prague would put their lives at grave risk. The reach and brutality of the Nazi police grew more pervasive each day, making any hope for safety in their home city impossible. With few options available, they determined that fleeing was their only chance for survival. After carefully considering the circumstances and the tightening grip of Nazi control, they concluded that France was the only feasible destination open to them at that time.

Rebecca recounted, with deep sorrow, that her family members chose to remain in Prague for their own personal reasons. Tragically, every member of her family was eventually captured by the Nazis and did not survive the Holocaust. On Hugo's side, the outcome was equally devastating: only his brother managed to escape the Nazi purge, surviving the horrors that claimed so many others. This profound loss weighed heavily on both Hugo and Rebecca as they continued their journey for survival, forever marked by the memories of those they lost.

Rebecca explained that in order for them to "get out of Prague," they needed to obtain forged passports. She recounted the process of how they managed to achieve this. With the risks growing each day under Nazi occupation and the increasing likelihood of being identified as Jews, possessing genuine documentation was impossible. Therefore, the only way forward was to rely on forged documents, which would provide them with a new identity and a chance at freedom.

Rebecca described how Hugo's father had learned of a contact named Mr. Josef Wiese, located in the Smichov district of Prague. This contact had a reputation for helping those in desperate situations by producing forged passports—for a steep price. The cost was approximately seven thousand koruna each. To raise the necessary funds, Hugo sold his valuable belongings, including his watch and violin, while Rebecca parted with her jewelry and other cherished possessions. She recalled how distressing it was to sell off nearly everything they owned, but their survival depended on it.

Time was of the essence. Their plan had to be carried out quickly and discreetly, as being caught by the Gestapo would have far more dire consequences. After gathering about 18,000 korunas, Hugo discreetly arranged a meeting with Josef at a local piano tavern where he regularly played. That evening, after his first set, Hugo joined Josef for a quiet conversation. They discussed the details, and Hugo passed Josef a music sheet containing all the necessary information for the forged documents. Josef estimated that it would take about three days to complete the work and agreed to accept half the payment upfront and the remainder upon delivery.

Three days later, they met again at a park bench overlooking the Vltava River. In a carefully orchestrated exchange, Josef handed Hugo a folded newspaper with the completed passports concealed inside, while Hugo left the remaining payment in a small paper bag. Without drawing attention to themselves, they went their separate ways. Upon returning home, Hugo and Rebecca inspected the passports and were relieved to find that Josef had done an excellent job; they were now disguised as non-Jewish German citizens.

A few days later, Hugo heard news of Josef was arrested and later was shot Infront of his own home by the Nazi police. What Hugo heard was that Josef was arrested for treason and resisted arrest. These instances were becoming more common, and they were concerned that an investigation of Nazi police of Josef home and his documents will be troublesome, as the Police might find information about them.

Hugo arranged to get out of Prague as soon as possible. Their situation was getting worse and dangerous as time passed by. It will be just a matter of time when they will be called out by local Nazi sympathizers and be arrested.

Their planning had to be precise, knowing how the detailed the Nazis ran their operations, they had to be careful. It took them a few days to plan their route and train schedules.

With each passing day their situation was getting worse, The Nazis had been taking control of most of the city, and all exits.

The day arrived, they both stared at their bare home, all their heirlooms vanished and they knew it would last time in their home.

They removed the Star of David Badge on their clothing. Suitcases in hand, they headed out, locked the door for the last time, and walked together down the staircase quietly. It was a cold, rainy day as they ventured into the streets.

As they made it to the concourse area of the train station, it was crowded and terribly busy, German soldiers patrolling some with their German Shepards constantly barking. As they continued to walk to the station entrance, Hugo told Rebecca to lower her hat and to avoid any eye contact to be inconspicuous as to avoid being recognized.

She was extremely nervous, but Hugo remained calm. As calm as a conductor on the podium starting a concerto. Hugo was a professional and knew how to keep his poise. He walked so calmly as if he was gliding.

They now had to pass through the Nazi checkpoints to get to the train platforms. Rebecca spotted a young soldier at one of the check point desks; he looked less intimidating than the other burly soldiers. She tugged on Hugo's arm and looked at him and looked at the young soldier. Without a word, Hugo understood. They both calmly headed to his line. The young German soldier looked at their Passports skeptically, his reaction was obviously concerning, Rebecca noticed this and with a confident stern voice said, "Schauen uns an, wir sind Ayran" (look at us, we are Aryan) "Siehst du nicht, wir sind Deutsch" (can you not see we are Germans). Her German was flawless, the young soldier shuttered for a second, hearing her perfect fluent German accent amidst the chaos hit a familiar tone to his ear. He stared at the passes carefully; Rebecca's demeanor remained confident and authoritative.

The young soldier then looked at her and then at Hugo from head to toe. Convinced by their overall appearance, he shrugged his head, gestured them to move on, confidently they walked through the train station check points.

The platform was in their sight as they walked calmly. Rebecca's heart was still pounding from the earlier incident. As the train rolled up on time, as soon as the door opened, a crowd of passengers started pushing and shoving to get on, people hastily boarded the train.

The stop at their station was brief, not more than fifteen minutes; Still people were fighting to get on. Rebecca and Hugo found seats and huge sigh of relief came over them. A few whistles blew from the locomotive and the train pulled from the Station.

Rebecca had to pause her story as the nurse's assistant walked in, Sonia, one of the old timers working at the hospital. Sonia is Colombian, in her mid-fifties, a genuinely nice lady. I have been acquainted with her for several years and have provided her with courtesy medical advice on multiple occasions, aware that she lacked medical insurance.

I greeted her "Hola" and asked how her day was going. "I'm doing ok doctor." I know she recently was dealing with the passing of her husband about a week ago. She delivered Rebecca her dinner and helped her to eat. I watched how patiently and gently she was while going through all the hardships of her family problems, I would have given her a medal for her commitment. Truly they are unsung heroes. Sonia aided her to the bathroom and cleaned her. She helped her lay back in bed, as she lay in bed she dozed off, and everything was lost. She was a blank page and had lost track of everything. The story telling would have to wait for another day.

The next day, as I finished my routine rounds and again, I would visit the rehabilitation unit last.

I did not really have any expectations and thought that Rebecca would not recall anything from yesterday. I woke her up from her nap, at first awakening she was groggy and confused. I asked her if she remembered her story from yesterday... she does not recall. I was not surprised as memory loss is quite common for dementia patients. I then ask her a few more general questions, then she suddenly recalls, "Ah I do remember." she recalls and she stares at me, I ask her, "do you remember what happened after you and your husband escaped from Prague". I am on the edge, hoping she remembers and does not fall back to her confused state. She pauses for a moment and continues her story...

---

*References

https://www.yadvashem.org, The world holocaust remembrance center.

https://www.nationalww2museum.org, The National WW II Museum.

https://encyclopedia.ushmm.org, The United States holocaust memorial museum.

Chapter 4

Escape to France.

It was a long train ride to France, the passengers on train all had a look of despair, silence, everyone kept to themselves. It was only the sound of the train rolling down the tracks.

Rebecca recalls Hugo telling her stories of his time at the Vienna state academy of art in Austria.

During this blissful period in his life, Hugo experienced one of his greatest joys: being accepted into the Vienna State Academy of Art, renowned as one of the world's most prestigious art schools. His admission marked a significant accomplishment, placing him among the select few with the talent and determination to study at such a distinguished institution.

At the academy, Hugo had the privilege of learning under some of the era's most esteemed conductors, composers, and professors. These mentors shaped his artistic development, offering invaluable instruction and insight into the world of fine arts and music. The environment fostered creativity, discipline, and a deep appreciation for both classical and contemporary approaches, making Hugo's time at the academy a cherished and formative chapter in his life.

Hugo recalls a story told by one of his professors about young fellow named "Adolf Hitler," several years earlier the young Hitler was walking on the very same campus.

He was aspiring to become a professional painter. Although for Hitler it was a much opposite experience. Hitler applied at the academy of arts in Vienna as well, but unfortunately, he failed to be accepted. The following year Hitler tried again and was rejected. Hugo told Rebecca, "If only they accepted him, the world would be a different place." Adolf Hitler's dream of being a painter was never to be. Instead, he went to Germany, enlisted in the Germany army, as private first class, served in World War one, after the war he went into politics.

Adolf Hitler would then paint a portrait of propaganda, antisemitism that eventually elevated himself to become chancellor.

After then Hitler eventually became Fuhrer of Germany, and the rest is history. *

Hugo sadly reminisced of his once prominent position; A man respected in his field of work, and in an instant, everything was lost. Now he is fleeing their home with nothing.

He told Rebecca how quickly "one's life can change." They had lost everything they had worked so hard for and in an instant, it was all gone. He was still optimistic and thought they still had each other and were still alive, unlike many other Jews that were left behind.

Rebecca held strong, she had faith, and she held Hugo and said, "Yahweh will provide," Hugo smirked, took a deep breath, stared at the distance through the frosted train window, His sad deep-set eyes said it all.

The train charged along the frosted tracks; it was a long train ride. The sway of the train put them both in a deep sleep, while the locomotive sped onward, crossing the heart of Germany towards Paris.

The trip was three and half days. There were several inspections and stopovers during the trip. Most of them in Germany. Dresden, Berlin, Hannover, and Dusseldorf to name a few. All inspections were daunting. The Third Reich soldiers would board with their German Shepards barking furiously while inspecting and checking everyone passports. Fortunately, they passed all the strict meticulous inspections expected by the of Germans Army.

Josef Wiese's handiwork was exceptional. As they got through every stop-over in Germany. As they crossed Belgium and into France a great sigh of relief came over them.

---

*References:

https://war-documentary.info

https://www.nationalww2museum.org, The National WW II museum.

https://encyclopedia.ushmm.org, The United States holocaust memorial museum.

Chapter 5

Paris.

The train crossed the border into France, at last, they have made it out of Germany, passing several French villages, solace came over them as the train headed on to the city of Paris.

Paris, renowned for its beauty, culture, and vibrancy. Rebecca and Hugo arrived at the bustling Gare de Lyon train station, a central hub teeming with people from across the continent. After a long and arduous journey, they stepped off the train, feeling the exhaustion from days of travel. The chill in the air only added to their discomfort, and hunger gnawed at them as they searched for relief.

Despite their longing for rest, warmth, and food, their immediate needs would have to wait. Before they could seek shelter or satisfy their hunger, Rebecca and Hugo first had to navigate the French immigration process, an essential step for all newcomers entering the city at that time.

At that time France officials were aware of the turmoil boiling in the eastern Europe, and overwhelmed with refugees coming from Germany, Poland, and other eastern countries in Europe.

consequently, the prevailing sentiment in France was far from welcoming.

Hugo and Rebecca both spoke fluent French which help their situation enormously. Again, acting calm and confidently they entered The French Immigration officers' counters, with confidence they presented their passports, overwhelmed with the rush of people from the train, the French officer looked at them and their passports, and what seemed a quick visual examination, he stamped their passports and yelled "nekst" and sent them on their way.

Hugo knew his way around Paris from his days playing small concertos during his youth. Hugo and Rebecca for the first time they felt abandon, alone and without a home, as like many Jews that left their home, they were fugitives who committed no crime. Hugo would seek out his good friend and a former colleague named Jean Moreau. He met Jean at the Music Academy in Vienna. Hugo played quartet with him on several occasions; Hugo knew him well, and they had been close friends ever since. As much of a burden it was on Jean, he had no other good options, and they were desperate, Hugo recalled Jean residence in the Latin Quarters. This part of Paris is known for its artistic atmosphere. They were desperate and took the chance to visit him and ask him for help.

Jean's address was about half an hour's walk from the train station. Rebecca was exhausted, she asks Hugo, "where do we go from here?"

Hugo glanced at her tired face, feeling despaired himself, but with an optimistic facial expression. He said, "I have a friend in Paris that might help us," Rebecca felt confident that Hugo would deliver as he always did.

After an exhausting walk, they got to Jean's address. It was late in the evening, in the dark, cold alleyway, tired and starving, Hugo composed himself, knocked on the heavy wooden door guarding the main entrance to a housing complex. A melodic voice from a window a few floors up said, "who's knocking there at this time of the night." Hugo recognized that lively voice. He responded in his low baritone voice, "Jean, it's me Hugo." Jean recognized that voice Immediately. Jean was ecstatic to see his good old friend. "Hugo, my friend is that you"! "Yes, indeed my friend it's me" Hugo answered. Jean was a true Frenchman; he was smaller in stature than Hugo, but with his dark hair and brown eyes, and chiseled facial features, he would stand out on any musical stage. Jean came running down to open the building's huge doors. Hugo introduced Rebecca; Jean joked how Hugo was able to marry someone so beautiful. And without any hesitation Jean rushed them inside. He gave them food and wine.

Jean, knowing Hugo very well, already had the sense of why Hugo was in Paris.

They talked mostly through the night, while Rebecca rested. They reminiscence their time together in college, the concertos they did, they laughed at they are mess-ups and boosted about their good performances. They talked about their former peers and teachers and eventually got to talk about the status of the war. Jean was a highly intelligent man, as was Hugo, they already knew what was on their minds without even directly talking about it.

Jean offered them a place to stay for the time being. His living space was exceedingly small; it would be sufficed for the time being. So begins their life in France.

Hugo would discard of their German passports; at the time Germans were not welcomed in France. They would have to go about with no documents and pretend to be French citizens.

They would not stay in Paris for long. With little money, no assured work, constantly worried of being arrested by the French police, resulted in constant feeling of anxiety for Rebecca and Hugo. Jean was able to introduce Hugo to few restaurants and pubs in Paris and Jean with multiple contact around the music scene He would have Hugo would fill in for position that open, being an astute multi-instrumentalist, Hugo would play guitar, percussion, piano and wind instruments like, the Saxophone or clarinet, whatever fill in's bands required.

Hugo's musical ability to play whenever and whatever instrument took notice amongst the Paris musical scene. Which landed him a permanent place in an upscale restaurant; he would play there on a regular basis, and his reputation grew. Eventually Hugo earned a decent amount of money, and Rebecca was able to find work in a Patisserie. It was here where she would learn to create pastries, cakes, and other French breads. With their combined income, they could afford to move out of Jean's place. With the deepest gratitude Hugo bid Jean, his old friend farewell.

They found a modest flat to rent in the North-eastern area of Paris, this area of the working-class neighborhood of Paris. The flat was also exceedingly small and was located on the fifth floor. To get there you would have to ride in a tiny elevator that carries a maximum of two people at a time. An old rusted retractable gate opened and closed which triggered the activation of the lift. The alternative way up was a dark spiral staircase that was about four feet wide at the end of the building. The latter was their choice most of the time.

In the lobby of the building sits the landlord, a well-dressed, full make-up, and manicured woman in her sixties', she sits all-day with her golden brown Pomeranian on her lap, constantly smoking and reminding the every tenant that passes by, that rent is due at the end of the week.

They also frequently visited the a nearby Synagogue every Shabbat. There they would meet new friends and obtain updates on what was going on the eastern side of Europe.

One day, Hugo left early to meet with the owner of a new tavern. Rebecca, upon waking up felt severely nauseated, she ran to the bathroom and had a violent vomiting episode.

As she sat on the cold tile bathroom floor and she realized one more thing. she was without a menstrual period for at least a two now. Emotionally scared, but she had mixed feelings about her suspicion.

Hugo came home late that evening, seeing Rebecca's facial expression, he knew something was wrong. That evening She would tell Hugo she suspects she is pregnant. He sat down and slumped on the floor.

They had to verify their suspicion; so they visited a nearby clinic. They registered and paid the fee up front and both sat anxiously in the waiting area.

"Rebecca Frolich" called the nurse, Rebecca was extremely nervous as she entered the foyer and into the examination room, the physician attended to her and a urine test was done followed by a physical and gynecological examination. Afterwards She came out sat in the waiting room with Hugo, silently they waited...

The Doctor came out, with a stoic demeanor, he said "congratulations you are three months pregnant." he smiled, shook Hugo's hand, and bid them "Adieu."

Rebecca looked at Hugo and without a word, they knew their lives had changed. A tear fell from Hugo's eyes. It was tears of joy and sadness, as he knew the challenges they would face in a time of uncertainty.

Chapter 6

Exodus

It had been nearly two years since Rebecca and Hugo departed from Prague. Now the news from Eastern Europe was deeply unsettling. The German army had invaded and occupied vast areas, advancing further into Russia. "Jews were being arrested and executed in every city and town. Most were taken to concentration camps," Rebecca recalled grimly. "They were marked with tattooed numbers on their arms to identify them." These remembrances illustrated the horrific hatred that the Nazi regime unleashed as they continued their relentless occupation, city by city.

By May 1940, the German Third Reich had invaded France, initially taking control of its northern region and extending into Paris. At this point, the German Wehrmacht had effectively occupied most of Northern France and the Atlantic coast.*

It had been almost two years since Rebecca and Hugo left Prague, now news from Eastern Europe has been Troubling, as the German army occupied most of eastern parts of Europe and was pushing onto Russia. "Jews in every city and town were being arrested, executed, most Jews

were and brought concentration camps" "they were tattooed numbers on their arms," to "identify them," as Rebecca recalls these were the horrors of hatred that the Nazi war machine brought with them as they raged on to occupy city after city.

The German Third Riech invaded France in May

1940, the Nazi forces of the war they initially occupied northern part of France, and into Paris. The Germany Wehrmacht now has occupied most of Northern and Atlantic coasts of France by this time*.

Rebecca recalls when the Nazis invaded Paris, they joined thousands of French refuges on their "Exodus" towards the south of France.

The journey was extremely hard, by train, buses, and on foot they pursued southward.

They stayed in refuge shelters, churches, or schools, and even farmhouses they found along the way.

Hugo and Rebecca moved further south of France deep into the unoccupied parts of the country. During their journey southward, they were in and out of Churches, private homes, farmhouses, and schools.

Most French villages were sympathetic to the refugees. After the defeat and Occupation of Germany, there was an armistice signed by Germany and France and the Collaborative Vichy Government was created.

The Vichy Government would govern most of the southern part of France.

The Vichy government was much lenient than the Nazi regime. The Vichy Government cared more for the French people and fleeing refuges.

Rebecca and Hugo initially were able posed as a French citizen since their French accents were both flawless. Claiming they lost all their documents during her evacuation to Paris. Food, medicine, and shelter were scarce. And now four months pregnant it made it more challenging, fortunately in some villages the French government gave out "rations" of food, milk, and other necessary supplies. During their journey south, Hugo was able to obtain false identity cards and ration cards from a priest that he helped repair the church's pipe organ.

Eventually they would reach and stay in the city of Lyons. They settled in the area's shelter facility provided by aid a humanitarian organization. *

Rebecca was able to find work in a textile factory during the day. Hugo was able to work as he played piano and entertained in local pubs and restaurants at night.

Once she would visit a Red Cross facility for a pregnancy check-up. The Red Cross was immensely helpful, she received gratuitous health care, and she was given a temporary "health pass card."

Hugo worked mainly for tips. As tavern owners could not afford to pay him a salary and would not employ him as he had no documents. It was tough, but most of the patrons loved him playing and tipped him very well.

As the war progressed the political landscape in France changed as well, towns eventually came under German Rule in collaboration with the local town's officials.

As the German army-imposed laws, the local town's official could not anything but follow them. Some of the proclamations was branding Jewish people as a third-class citizen.

The established French-Jewish people were not allowed to own property or businesses. Also, any French establishment employing or even harboring a Jewish employee was against Nazi rules.

They continue to survive in hiding and posing as French refuges for the meantime.

---

*References:

https://www.bbc.co.uk;https://yadvashem.org

https://www.jewishvirtuallibrary.org.

https://war-documentary.info;

https://francetoday.com;

https://encyclopedia.ushmm.org

https://www.observatoire-humanitaire.org;

Chapter 7

Delivery.

Rebecca recalls; she was more than nine months pregnant as she continued working at the textile factory, working six days a week consisting of strenuous manual labor overall. One Friday afternoon as the factory was closing, she suddenly felt a stabbing pain in her abdomen. It lasted about three minutes, she brushed it off, then ten minutes later the same pain happened, now lasting about five minutes. her first pregnancy, she had no idea what to do and expect. She remembered the education she got from the Clinic at the French Red cross. Rebecca was going into labor, for her she suddenly felt very anxious and scared, she sat down on floor then she suddenly felt a warm feeling running down her inner thighs, she looked down and saw a streak of blood running down both of her thighs, she was bleeding out.

There was a German sergeant patrolling the factory, who actually has been there some time and had an infatuation with on Rebecca, fortunately who was in the vicinity at the time, He knew Rebecca was in trouble and despite breaking his duty and guard patrol he carried her into one of the military trucks and rushed her to the nearby hospital, she gotten there in

just in time. The Sargent will pay the price and would be reprimanded by his superior.

On arrival she was going into shock from blood loss. Rebecca was pale as a ghost and was losing consciousness rapidly.

On staff was the town's Physician, Dr. Michelle, recognizing the severity of her condition, He rushed her in, fortunately there was one operating room available, as during the war most hospitals were overwhelmed with war-related injuries. Dr. Michelle had to act quick; she underwent an emergency cesarean section. She lost a lot of blood and was in critical condition. The baby was in good health with no issues. Rebecca sustained a ruptured placenta but will survive the ordeal. If not for the German solider and his quick actions and the skill of Dr. Michelle, she and her baby would not have survived.

During the war, numerous Jewish pregnant refugees faced unfortunate circumstances, with many mothers losing their lives due to birth-related complications. In situations where no family members were available, the French Red Cross and the Children's Aid Rescue Society arranged for the children to be placed in a network of protected homes or sent to orphanages In time, some children were reunited with relatives.*

It took her two weeks to recover from her blood loss and from the stress of the delivery. She recovered with no major complication and was able to hold her baby for the first time.

As Rebecca and her baby thrived with the exceptional care of two French Red Cross nurses, sisters named, Yvette and Marie. The two sisters fell in love with a "very cute baby," said Rebecca.

The hospital conditions were harsh, with hundreds of patients, lack of sanitation was most of the challenge, but the two nurses made an extra effort to care for Rebecca and her baby.

Hugo would visit in the late evenings or before the break of dawn but would not stay long as the hospital was full of French police and German soldiers. Rebecca named her daughter Hannah, both continued to improve, and were discharged back to the shelter.

As time passed by, Yvett and Marie became close to both Rebecca and Hugo and a friendship developed.

Suzette and Marie introduced Rebecca and Hugo to their father, named Mr. Nicolas Laroche who was the mayor of a small village just south of Lyons, Laroche instinctively knew the couple were Jewish, but her never said a word.

Over the coming months they were frequently invited to Laroche's home, the two sisters adored Hannah, especially watching her grow up.

Hugo played music for the mayor's parties and gave piano lessons to Marie who loved to play the piano. In time they became like a "second family"

Laroche was a generous man, he found trust and saw the goodness in Hugo, he offered them to stay in one of his old farmhouses just outside the village. Rebecca and Hugo gladly accepted, Laroche knew he was taking a huge risk harboring Jewish refugees.

Laroche also introduced Hugo to one of his friends, Jaques Dubuisson, who owned a restaurant called "Le Brasserie." The restaurant was connected to a big hotel situated on the outskirts of Lyons. As long as he stays inconspicuous, they will be fine.

Hugo started playing at La Brasserie and he was well accepted, as a seasoned musician, and had a vast repertoire of standard French, Italian, and English pieces.

Each night, Hugo entertained patrons by playing piano and occasionally handling vocals. The locals loved his performances and often came just to experience Hugo performance.

They called him "Le Maestro." More came to the restaurant, and business was good. They incorporated a local French singer named Suzzette Granier, a voluptuous Burnette beauty with the most exotic green eyes, her aura was as stunning as her angelic voice. The two complimented each other perfectly, with her Melodic French voice and Hugo's virtuoso playing it was the perfect blend of harmony. In time she developed an infatuation with Hugo. Rebecca knew this and said Hugo he "kept it professional."

The restaurant was packed every night, with people often waiting in line outside for a table. Between the restaurant's exceptional dining and outstanding entertainment, it was a successful symbiotic partnership. This was good for Jaques, but in the back of Hugo's mind he knew that this might not be the best thing for him...

---

*References

https://encyclopedia.ushmm.org

https://wwv.yadvashem.org

Chapter 8

Narrow Escape.

Rebecca still in a state of lucidity, as she continues her story telling, she pauses and says "this the most dangerous moment" she goes on and continues...

It was a Friday night, she got back from work exhausted, she had dinner with Hannah and Hugo. Hugo finished the evening chores and tucked Hannah in bed; He kissed Rebecca goodbye as he went off to work.

It was a peaceful evening when Hugo set off on his walk to work. Just a few steps from the restaurant, a soldier suddenly emerged from a shadowy alley, barking, "Halt!" Hugo felt a chill run down his spine at the sound. The soldier demanded to see his papers. Panic surged within him—he didn't have his pass on him. As he fumbled through his coat, searching for an excuse, the soldier was on the verge of taking him into custody. Just then, Jaques's voice pierced through the tension: "Stop! He works for me!" The soldier glanced at Jaques, recognizing him from past encounters. Jaques had often been generous with meals and drinks for the German troops, which had earned him a certain level of respect.

Jaques came over and vouched for him and explained that Hugo worked for him at the restaurant as the pianist. The soldier looked at Jaques, shook his head and held his rifle gesturing towards the restaurant. Jaques nodded as a sign of gratitude to the German, and they both headed to the restaurant. Jaques was quiet, Hugo wanted to say something but as they approached the restaurant, Jaques did not need to explain.

As Hugo gazed up at the Hotel, he was met with an unexpected sight. The restaurant's sign, Le Brasserie, was obscured by a large banner proclaiming "Soldat hiem" — soldiers' home. Red swastika flags hung ominously from the hotel façade. His heart raced as he and Jacques exchanged a glance, a silent understanding passing between them. A handful of German soldiers stood guard outside the restaurant. Hugo struggled to steady his breath; his heart pounded as though he had just sprinted a marathon. That brief walk from the street to the restaurant steps felt like an arduous mile. Once they stepped inside, the situation escalated. They were confronted by a crowd of at least two hundred men and women — a chaotic mix of enlisted soldiers, officers, and collaborating French police.

The restaurant was packed. Jaques whispered, "A Panzer Division moved in today and most of them are housed in the Hotel. "They took over the restaurant this evening, and that's why I was outside trying to get to you beforehand," "It is too late now," "just do your routine with Suzzette and try not to attract to much attention."

The crowd was loud, drinking, singing, as most of them were intoxicated. One stood stoic, the commander of the army division, Colonel Muller, a battle-hardened Wehrmacht Officer.

The seasoned musician was a bundle of nerves as he tried to lighten the mood, quipping to Jaques, "It's just like my first recital." With a sea of Nazi faces staring at him, he found himself in an unsettling situation, particularly as a Jew. Fortunately, by his side that evening was the stunning Suzette, the charismatic host and singer who effortlessly commanded the stage.

Hugo got up on stage, took one deep breath, and started playing. He kept the tempo to a minimum to avoid too much attention. Hugo knew how to control his audience. With the help of Suzette's showmanship, the maestro and the siren lured the unwary crowd to a state of tranquility. As they played on, during the middle of their set, Hugo could not help but notice one soldier staring at him intently all night. Hugo would glimpse at him periodically; he did not want to make eye contact. He felt something was off. His heart skipped a beat as he recognized who the soldier was. He missed a note, not expected from a professional caliber musician, Susette could not help but glanced at Hugo, and he winched at her, acknowledging his mistake, He recovered and played on. It was Thomas Lischka, his old-time friend from Prague. Thomas is now a Czech conscript in the German army.

Hugo and Thomas shared a close friendship during their teenage years. As Hugo observed, a man with the rank of Captain—a burly SS officer with deep-set eyes and thin lips—sat beside Thomas. His strong, hardened face exuded an intimidating presence.

Hugo recognizes him, his name was Krause Wolfgang. He was a bully in school, Krause also from their hometown in Prague. Hugo remembers this boy was not of the ordinary, he recalls, he had a "killer instinct" and had a history of violence. In school, Krause once got into a fight, where he assaulted another boy using his drumsticks, the other boy was hospitalized and barely survived. Hugo knew this man spelled trouble and was high dangerous.

Hugo looked back during their school days; Thomas was his best friend at one time. They would skip school together and hang out in Thomas's backyard as they would climb this big apple tree, they picked and ate the apples, as they talked about anything and everything teenagers did back then. Time passed by and they went their separate ways after school.

As Hugo went to the College in Vienna, Thomas went to another college in Prague.

Two years later, Thomas was accepted and made the move to the same college in Vienna. He and Hugo had a chance to reconnect, albeit briefly. Their initial excitement and happiness at seeing each other was palpable. On one particular event night, Hugo extended an invitation to Thomas to join a party. Hugo picked up Thomas from his quarters, and the two headed to the event happening in one of the college halls. As they made their way there, Hugo spotted some friends and felt a surge of excitement to introduce them to Thomas. Unlike Hugo's glamorous and dashing presence, Thomas was shorter with a sturdier build. When Hugo introduced him to his friends, they all seemed quite similar—tall, handsome, and dressed in modish outfits. They greeted Thomas with a handshake but quickly turned their attention back to chatting and joking with Hugo, leaving Thomas feeling somewhat sidelined. It was awkward for both of them; Hugo wanted Thomas to be part of his friend group, but it was clear that Thomas didn't quite fit in, making the situation uncomfortable for everyone.

As the years went by, Hugo and Thomas gradually grew distant. Thomas started to form a new circle of friends, while Hugo found himself caught up in the enjoyment of his own group. Deep down, Hugo felt a twinge of guilt for letting Thomas down, but he couldn't bring himself to change his ways at that moment. This only fueled a sense of bitterness in Thomas toward Hugo. Eventually, time passed, and they lost touch completely.

Now Thomas and Hugo's paths have crossed again.

Hugo noticed that Thomas had recognized him, and Krause quickly sensed this.

Hugo had to do something; the last thing he wanted was Thomas or Krause to call him out on stage. Hugo, the maestro, took charge of the moment, cranking up the energy as he played with vigor—loud and fast. Suzette had no choice but to keep pace with him. She narrowed her eyes at him, but he simply nodded, urging her to join in the rhythm he had unleashed. He pounded the piano keys with fervor, the instrument seemed to respond in kind, reflecting the intensity of his performance. Suzette delivered a vocal spectacle unlike any other, her voice soaring above the fray. Under the sway of the liquor and the electrifying music, everyone—Thomas and Krause included—was blissfully unaware of anything beyond the moment

Colonel Muller calmly watched from the back of the dining hall and took note of Hugo's masterful skill.

After the chaos tapered down, Thomas in his drunkenness and still holding on to the bitterness of the past, told Krause "Do you recognize him," as Thomas pointed towards Hugo, Krause said "no." He uttered in his slurred speech "that's Hugo, my old Jewish friend from Prague". Wolfgang did not remember or cared to him, Hugo was nothing more than a Jew—a label that sparked no recollection or concern. His views were a reflection of deep-seated beliefs, thoroughly shaped by Nazi propaganda. And Krause was going after him at all cost.

Krause was also known for his brutality, and he was notorious for hunting down Jews and the French resistance fighters.

In a moment of sobriety Thomas felt quite guilty and thought to himself "what have I done."

Krause approached Colonel Muller and leaned in to whisper, "The piano player is a Jew." Colonel Muller remained impassive, seemingly uninterested in apprehending anyone at that moment. Instead, he felt a surge of irritation towards Krause for interrupting him after such an enjoyable performance. With a furrowed brow, Muller took a moment to reflect on the situation.

As the commanding officer he had his duties and orders from the high command, he said, "we will investigate first thing in the morning." Krause was extremely disappointed and frustrated. But as a subordinate to the Colonel, he really could not do anything.

After Hugo finished playing, he inconspicuously made his way to the back of the restaurant and through the cleaning storage area, as he tried to leave via the back doors. He peaked out the door and saw two soldiers smoking in the back alley. Suzette spotted him leaving, and she followed him to the back room, she was hoping to be alone with Hugo. But as she saw Hugo in a panic trying to leave, she suddenly understood. She snuck up behind Hugo; he was startled momentarily but relived when he saw it was Suzette. He peaked again through the back door; the alley was still guarded by the two troopers. Suzzette whispered a plan, she would distract the two soldiers while Hugo would slip down the opposite way of the alley. Hugo knew she was taking a huge risk for him. Turns out was secretly part of the French resistance and she would help anyone who was not on the side of the Nazis.

He looked at her intently and kissed her on her forehead. They looked at each other and knew this was farewell.

Suzette came out of the back door and called the two soldiers; she seductively asked to light her cigarette. The two soldiers had no chance to resist the sirens' command. As the two Troppers walked towards Suzette, joking each other as they competed to offer her their lighters, she flirted with the two Germans which gave Hugo the chance to escape out of the back door and down the opposite way of the alley.

He cut through the fields, it was muddy, cold and he had to cross over several creeks, he ignored everything, his focus was to get to the farmhouse alive. He got to the farmhouse; he was drenched and covered in mud. Rebecca woke up, surprised, "what happened to you." Exhausted and trying to catch his breath, he held Rebecca's shoulders tight and said, "We must go now!"

They quickly packed their bags and went straight to Laroche's home for help. Laroche knew exactly what was happening, as he was aware of the Panzer Division that suddenly moved in and occupied the town that day. Laroche didn't waste any time; he took them out of town that very night. Their journey would lead them to an outlying area close to the French Alps, a quaint village nestled on the Larzac plateau.

Colonel Muller had a distinguished career as an army officer long before the Nazis came to power in Germany. His dedication lay with the German army. He also nurtured a profound appreciation for the arts and music. Deep down, Muller harbored significant disagreements with many of the Nazi policies, but he had to keep these opinions to himself. Any hint of dissent against the Fuhrer would be seen as treason, and he knew that would lead him straight to the unforgiving Russian front. Thus, he felt compelled to display unwavering loyalty to the Nazi mission in the presence of his men.

Colonel Muller found himself with no option but to face Jaques the next morning. Colonel Muller, accompanied by a couple of SS officers and four soldiers, including Thomas, returned to the restaurant.

Jaques met them at the entrance and already knew what the visit was about. Colonel Muller shouted in his deep husky voice "There is a Jew playing in your restaurant!" Jaques, he tried to downplay the situation by playing coy and claims he had no idea Hugo was a Jew. All he knew was he was a French refugee from Paris, but one of the SS officers insisted and said, "bring him to me I will find out in a second if he is a Jew."

The SS officer stated, "I will pull down his pants to find out," alluding to the fact that all Jewish males were circumcised. Jaques said he would find Hugo and bring him to the German headquarters as soon as possible.

The Colonel stood towering over Jaques warned him if he found out that he was as harboring any Jews, he would not hesitate to arrest him and his family and shut down his business.

The colonel clicked his heels, casting one last glance at the piano on the stage and throwing a sharp look at Jaques, who wore a subtle smirk. With a measured gaze around the room, he turned to his men and strode out, leaving a silence in his wake.

Colonel Muller appreciated Hugo's talent, and he would not pursue hunting Hugo down, instead he would distract his subordinates with other "Important matters." When Krause heard of this, he was furious and vowed to hunt down this "Jew."

---

*References:

https://holocaustmusic.ort.org

http://www.holocaustresearchproject.org

Chapter 9

Larzac Plateau.

Rebecca's story continues; she said they "traveled a long way" and reached a place called "Larzac."

The Larzac Plateau, located in the southeastern part of France, it has a mountainous terrain, with deep gorges, caves, lakes, and underground rivers. It is accessible by a narrow winding uphill road. On the Larzac Plateau, there are several towns dating back to the 12th century, towns consisting of medieval architecture, castle buildings, cobble stone roads, and alley ways.

Laroche drove them up to a small village, called La Couvertoirade on the Larzac plateau, it was surround by a defensive stone wall built by Knights Templar that founded the village centuries ago. In the village, small stone houses next to each other, in center of this compact village sits a large cathedral. Surrounding the village was a gorge and dry grassland. *

At the time, the village residents were mostly farmers, and sheep herders. Due to the isolated location; it was suitable for many French resistance fighters to take refuge in the village.

Laroche knew the priest that presided in the village, named Father Pierre. Laroche had known him for years as both were once schoolmates. Laroche would ask his good friend for an enormous favor.

Father Pierre, a man of God, warmly welcomed the family and took them in. Larcohe bid them farewell, as he would need to get back the Lyons soon to before the Germans get suspicious of him.

They would stay in one of the chambers beneath the cathedral. They would be safe for the time being.

Hugo fixed, fine-tuned the cathedral's pipe organ. He would fill the air with his music during masses and various village gatherings, bringing joy and a splash of color to those dark times.

Father Pierre and the villagers were truly delighted by the refreshing shift in the atmosphere during the masses.

Rebecca would help in Father Pierre's kitchen, cooking and baking and bringing flavor to the ministry's gatherings. Father Pierre would bring them rations of milk and meat mostly donated by the villagers.

In late spring of 1944, a British pilot conducting reconnaissance over the Larzac area faced an unexpected attack from a small, isolated German tank unit. Despite the surprise assault, he managed to eject from his aircraft and successfully deployed his parachute. The plane glided a few miles before crashing against the mountainside. Unfortunately, the pilot sustained injuries and lost consciousness upon landing.

Fortunately, he was rescued by a group of French resistance fighters who were on patrol nearby.

The small German tank unit would stay in place, awaiting reinforcement from the north. as they were under constant sabotage attacks by the resisting French.

The British pilot was brought to La Couvertoirade and hidden also in the cathedral. He recovered after a few days. A meeting was held in the cathedral with the French resistance and the British pilot. Rebecca and Hugo overheard the British pilot saying there will be a large Allied in invasion coming very soon.

In a matter of days, and news over the radio of the Americans and Allies have landed and taken over the beaches of Normandy and are pushing in land. A sign of hope, as the villagers rejoiced. But the battles have not ended yet.

The Americans and the Allied forces, together with the French resistance waged fierce battles, as each town, village and city was being liberated.

In the south of France, in Lyons, Colonel Muller's Division was defeated and his regiment dispersed. A remaining army unit now under the command of Krause retreated southeast and would rally up with the small German Tank unit in the Larzac area.

Krause heard from his sources that many villages in the Larzac area are harboring Jewish families, and he had a strong feeling Hugo was hiding in one of the villages.

Thomas was still serving under Krause's unit as they mobilized southeast.

Krause received an intelligence report that British pilot survived the plane crash and was brought to La Courertiorade. Krause now would organize a convoy and head towards La Couvertoirade.

On a warm summer morning a young French scout from the village spotted and alerted he village of a German convoy coming up the mountain pass, this was Krauses unit.

Rebecca vividly remembers this terrifying sight. Hurriedly they grabbed their belongings and young Hannah planned for an escape. Rebecca was terrified and thought this was "the end." As there was no time to escape as the convoy raced up the mountain pass. But for some miracle the lead truck of the convoy broke down. And blocked the steep one-way road. This gave him time to run and hide; they ran for the cathedral and down a network of tunnels and the chambers.

After Pushing the truck off the road, the convoy started up again. It was a fury of gun fire and tank fire rained on the village. Troopers followed in and were going house to house looking for resistant fighters.

The Germans found the British operative and a group of resistant fighters hiding in a cathedral, a fierce gun fight was put up.

Rebecca and Hugo hid in the cathedral's crypt and followed a tunnel that led towards the fields.

The French resistance fighters were outnumbered and out powered by the German army.

The British operative and the French resistant fighters continued battling and gave an intense fight. They hid in a bunker beside the cathedral. The Nazi's eventually bombarded the bunker and flooded it and drowning them.

Krause entered and descended along the narrow tunnels and reached the cathedral's chambers like a predator stalking his prey. Hugo signaled for Rebecca and Hannah to move forward while he stayed back to keep Krause occupied. Knowing the labyrinthine tunnels well, he created a distraction by banging on the steel gates, which provided Rebecca and Hannah the precious moments they needed to slip away to the fields and find a hiding spot.

Krause finally caught up with Hugo, he ran as fast as his this weary legs could manage, he made it out of the tunnel and to the fields, Krause saw him and followed him to edge of the tunnel, Krause stood there and gently pulled out his German luger and slowly took aim. Hugo looked back for a split second, and bang! Hugo thought he was shot.

Hugo saw Krause fall face forward and then saw a figure emerging from the darkness of the tunnel. It was Thomas who held his rifle as smoke emanated from the barrel.

Thomas and Hugo locked eyes, and in that fleeting moment, an unspoken understanding passed between them. Suddenly, the silence shattered as a hail of gunfire tore into Thomas from behind. The remaining German soldiers, paralyzed by disbelief, turned their weapons on him after witnessing their leader succumb to the treachery of one of his own. In shock, they momentarily abandoned their pursuit of Hugo, unable to process the swift betrayal that had unfolded before them.

Hugo reunited with Rebecca and Hannah, and the trio sought refuge in the fields, remaining hidden until dawn. The German forces eventually withdrew from the village, retreating back towards Germany. A few days later, the American and allied troops arrived, filling the village with joy. In that moment of celebration, Hugo embraced Rebecca and Hannah, exclaiming, "We are free!"

---

*Reference:

https://lacouvertoirade.com

https://www.tourisme-aveyron.com/

https://www.data.gouv.fr/en

Chapter 10

Post-War.

In France, as the war began to deescalate, law and order broke down significantly. Even though the Vichy government declared antisemitic laws void, Jewish people still faced immense challenges. They grappled with the aftermath of war, dealing with trauma, homelessness, poverty, unemployment, and persistent prejudice. *

Many of their homes were destroyed, leaving them with nothing and forcing them to face an uncertain and difficult future.

Hugo, Rebecca, and Hannah would stay in France after the war. Hugo would find sporadic work. After the war there was not much work for a professional musician to go by.

They immigrated to the United States, sponsored by Rebecca's cousin. They first arrived in New York via a transatlantic ocean liner. At the time there were specific refugee Acts done by the US government, to help fleeing immigrants from Europe allocate visas and assisted in employment opportunities. * The couple has a new addition to their family, another daughter. Eventually Hugo found a music professor job in Ohio in the late 1950's. They eventually moved down to Florida. Hugo taught at the for some local colleges for a few years. *

They would settle down and retire in Central Florida. After Hugo's death, Rebecca, said she has lived alone in an independent living facility, as one of her daughters lived nearby and her other daughter lived out of state.

Her neighbors and the facility staff loved and admired her for her personality and her baking skills; she would make homemade goodies from time to time and share them with the community; these were fonder memories of her days in central Florida. *

She wrapped up her story for the day, and I encouraged her to take some time to rest, promising to return tomorrow. Her captivating tale left a lasting impression on me, and I expressed my gratitude for her time and for sharing such an extraordinary narrative. Before leaving the hospital that afternoon, I felt compelled to capture her words. I rushed to one of the nurses' stations, catching the curious gazes of the nurses as I hastily grabbed a piece of paper and began to jot down everything I could remember. I've heard countless World War Two stories, but this one was truly one of a kind.

Many stories from the Holocaust carry a poignant theme, which is completely understandable. However, Rebecca's story stands out in a unique way. It embodies themes of perseverance, patience, courage, loyalty, and faith. The most important takeaway is the reminder that we are all human. Despite our differences in religion, race, education, and culture, there exists both good and bad in every individual. We should strive to evaluate people based on their actions rather than their outward appearances.

---

*Reference:

https://www.tracesofwar.com

https://www.orlandosentinel.com

https://www.rescue.org

Chapter 11

Departure.

The next day, I wrapped up my rounds a bit early and hurried over to the Inpatient-Rehab unit to check on Rebecca. Overall, her recovery seemed to be progressing, albeit slowly.

"Good afternoon, Ms. Frolich," I greeted her, but she simply stared back at me, expressionless. I posed a few questions, but her responses were all off-topic. In an attempt to connect, I tried speaking to her in German, hoping it might spark some recognition. Unfortunately, she continued to look at me blankly. It was disheartening to realize she didn't remember me or recall the conversation we had the day before. I was not surprised by her regression to her prior mental state, as this was common.

My week-long shift had just wrapped up, and that was the last moment I saw Rebecca. It had only been a week since I spoke with the hospital's discharge manager about her situation. She kindly retrieved her notes, mentioning that Rebecca had been discharged from the rehab unit and that one of her daughters had taken her to "somewhere out on the west coast."

A few weeks later I gave her daughter Hannah a courtesy call. I was sad to hear that she passed away. Hannah said she passed away, weeks after she moved out west. She did not go into detail. I gave her my condolences and that was the last I will from her Hannah.

For many years I could not forget her story. I never forgot her saying "the world should know of my story" and "what we had to endure".

I can only speculate on why she chose to keep her story to herself. Perhaps it was the haunting memory of having to leave her family in Prague, a tragedy too painful to revisit. Or maybe it was guilt that held her back. The truth remains a mystery we'll never uncover.

Occasionally, I would think, how will I ever fulfill my promise. I knew it was a long shot, but I tried and reached out to a famous actor, I messaged him on his Instagram account about making Rebecca's story to turn into a movie, to my surprise he did message me back, although he said he had "too much" on his hands at that time.

I pondered; the only way I can get this out there is to turn this into a novel or a short story.

I had no writing skills or experience, English was not even my first language, the idea of putting her story into actual book took was far from a reality to me, so the idea took backseat for many years.

One day, I met a patient I'll refer to as Mr. L. He was in his late eighties, a genuinely kind man whom I admitted to the hospital. While his health wasn't in great shape, his mind remained remarkably sharp. As is my practice, I like to get to know my patients beyond their medical conditions. So when I asked him about his past career, he revealed that he was an author. He told me he had written a few books, and that struck a chord with me. Suddenly, like a ghost haunting me, I remembered Rebecca story.

I did look up Mr. L. online and I did find some of his published novels. The following day after treating him, we had another lengthy conversation, He told me more about his life and another thing that surprised me was he said that he was "Jewish," although he converted to Christian after he married.

I told him about my encounter with Rebecca and a summary of her story, and if he can help me turn it into an actual book. His face lit up and his depressed mood was instantly vanished

We talked more about Rebecca's story and the more he was interested. I was starting to get excited as well. He told me how we could collaborate and be co-authors, this idea got me interested again.

I thought this could be it, my promise to Rebecca might happen.

Unfortunately, while he was in the hospital his health slowly deteriorated. Mr. L's condition worsened to the point he would not be able to pursue writing the book and that idea of collaborating with him never came to fruition.

Although his advice inspired me to get this book started. I did take on the challenge of writing the truly beautiful story and Rebecca's remarkable story to life.

I researched extensively, asked people who have authored books, I did get some good advice, but others were discouraging.

As a Physician writing and publishing a book was particularly daunting. Juggling the responsibilities of caring for hundreds of chronically ill individuals while being on call around the clock posed an immense challenge.

As a creator, I often find myself needing to shift my mindset, stepping into a different time and place. This transition can be quite challenging. Being a physician makes it even harder to break free from analytical thought and embrace a more artistic approach. The process is almost surreal. There are moments when I dive into writing, fully immersed in a creative and imaginative space, only to be jolted back to reality by a call about a patient's emergency. In an instant, I have to turn off that creative flow and adopt a scientific perspective. It's frustrating because that interruption can disrupt my momentum, causing the story to lose its rhythm.

With time, I became accustomed to the challenges. Through patience and perseverance, as well as embracing a flexible mindset, the pieces of this story began to take shape. In the end, I completed it.

Chapter 12

Conclusion

I would like to mention a few more stories that are important for the current generation.

I still remember my grandfather's stories from a generation not too far away, a generation that experienced terrors of World War Two.

I can recall his tales of how he fought alongside the Americans during the war in the pacific against the Japanese in the Philippines Islands. His experiences of the brutally of war, including the infamous "Death March" of Bataan, were 75,000 American and Filipino POWs were forced to march more than sixty-five miles in horrid and scorching heat.

Thousands perished on the roadside. His life's story will soon to be forgotten, along with many others that perished during that war. *

Another sad story was from my wife's grandmother, were the during the occupation of the Japanese army, of a town called Los Banos, in the province of Laguna. Were one of the most beautiful girl in town was publicly humiliated by have her walk naked down main street, and afterwards molested.

This encourages us to take a step back and reflect on our current challenges. When we compare our lives to the difficulties faced in the past, it helps us gain a clearer perspective on our situation today.

In line of all the atrocities and lesson we should learn, another story comes to mind, this is from another patient of mine, will call him Mr. M., a 101-year-old man, who severed in World War Two as a crew member of the Berlin airlift. At the time I met him he was on his way to France, to pay tribute to the 80th anniversary of the Normandy D-day landing, as he was telling me his experiences there on the battle fields of France and Germany, he broke down in tears in his eyes, as he recalled his "I saw a lot of my friends die right beside me".

He also recalls the horrors of "the concentration camps." As his unit liberated the prisoners there, he said "it was unbelievable what we saw there."

"They were Real (the Concentration Camps), the people today who deny the camps were not real and are living on a different planet." Mr. M stated.

It has not even been one hundred since the fascist regimes of World War Two took millions of lives and left millions of people in suffering. Yet here we are, in our current generation, a lot of people are already denying Holocaust ever happened and atrocities by the evilest regimes that ruled the planet are fading away.

There are thousands of stories about World War two and the Holocaust, to which makes this book seems like a drop in a vast ocean, but it is one drop that exists. May this story live on and serve as a window to the past and beacon for the future. Thank you to all who helped make this story happen.

The End.

---

*References:

https://www.nationalmuseum.af.mil

Notes:

Dr. Arca grew up in the Philippines in a town where a US Naval Station once existed. It closed in the 1970's, many of the military and civilian personnel working on the base stayed, hence the town was heavily influenced by American culture. He earned his medical degree at De La Salle University in the Philippines in 1996 and Immigrated to the US in 1999, lived in Detroit, Michigan for a while before moving to Florida for his residency at the University of Florida in 2002.

He and his family moved to Orlando, Florida as it was ideal for its location and raising a family. He Served in US Air Force Medical Corps in Homestead, Florida and worked in Urgent care and as a Hospitalist for several years prior to building his own practice.

Dr Arca is the medical director of several long-term care facilities in Central Florida and does a lot of charity work for the underprivileged. Also participates in teaching Medical students and Nurse practitioners in the Orlando area colleges.

Prior to the pandemic, he had traveled extensively throughout Europe, Asia, the Middle East, and the Americas.

As an art enthusiast, interests are music, philosophy and painting. Creative writing is a new endeavor, and Le Maestro is his first publication.

www.ingramcontent.com/pod-product-compliance
Lightning Source LLC
Chambersburg PA
CBHW032210040426
42449CB00005B/525